NIGHT SCHOOL

ALSO BY CARL DENNIS

POETRY

A House of My Own
Climbing Down
Signs and Wonders
The Near World
The Outskirts of Troy
Meetings with Time
Ranking the Wishes
Practical Gods
New and Selected Poems 1974–2004
Unknown Friends
Callings
Another Reason

PROSE

Poetry as Persuasion

Carl Dennis

NIGHT SCHOOL

PENGUIN POETS

PENGUIN BOOKS

An imprint of Penguin Random House LLC
375 Hudson Street
New York, New York 10014
penguin.com

LIBRARY OF CONGRESS CATALOGING-IN-PUBLICATION DATA
Names: Dennis, Carl, author.
Title: Night school / Carl Dennis.
Description: New York : Penguin Books, [2018] | Series: Penguin poets
Identifiers: LCCN 2017041780 (print) | LCCN 2017043205 (ebook) |
ISBN 9780525504337 (ebook) | ISBN 9780143132356 (paperback)
Subjects: | BISAC: POETRY / American / General.
Classification: LCC PS3554.E535 (ebook) | LCC PS3554.E535 A6 2018 (print) |
    DDC 811/.54—dc23
LC record available at https://lccn.loc.gov/2017041780

Printed in the United States of America
10 9 8 7 6 5 4 3 2 1

Set in Garamond 3 LT Pro
Designed by Sabrina Bowers

To the memory of my brother Robert Dennis,

true teacher, true friend, and to the

memory of our brother Aaron

Acknowledgments

Thanks are due to the editors of the following magazines in which some of these poems first appeared:

The American Poetry Review ("At the Graveyard," "Favorite God," "Finding Thoreau," "Joseph's Work," "Nothing," "To the People of 2060," and "To Whitman")

Café ("Old Composer")

Five Points ("Old Story")

Colorado Review ("A Proposal")

Literary Matters ("Babel")

Muse ("Hunters")

New Letters ("On the Radio," "Power," "A Stand of Cottonwood")

The New Yorker ("Two Lives")

Ploughshares ("A Letter")

Salmagundi ("Crosstown Bus," "Help from an Old Critic," and "On the Beach")

This manuscript has benefited greatly from careful readings by several critical friends: Charles Altieri, Thomas Centolella, Alan Feldman, Mark Halliday, Tony Hoagland, Philip Schultz, and Emily Wheeler.
"Old Story" is for Robert Daly.

Contents

I

A Stand of Cottonwood   3

Fast Food   5

Bad Days, Good Days   7

Know Yourself   9

Joseph's Work   11

Blind Guest   13

Two Lives   14

In the Woods   17

To Earth   19

An Actress   20

My Defender   21

II

Table   25

A Proposal   27

Clippers   28

Power   30

A Friend and a Book   31

A History of Nagging   33

In the Moment   35

Not Description   37

A Letter   38

A Typescript   40

At the Graveyard   42

Emily's Birthday   43

III

On the Beach 47

Crosstown Bus 49

To the People of 2060 51

Favorite God 53

A Traveler from Altruria 55

When 57

Doe 59

Nothing 60

Wallace Siner 61

Tents and Houses 63

Hunters 65

Evening with Washington 67

IV

Finding Thoreau 71

Mrs. Gottlieb's Course in World Literature 72

Help from an Old Critic 74

At Emily Dickinson's House 75

Babel 76

On the Radio 78

Another Horatio 80

Old Composer 81

To Whitman 83

A Landscape 86

Old Story 87

NIGHT SCHOOL

I

A Stand of Cottonwood

I'm glad to be here, amid these cottonwood trees,
Feeling the wind from the lake on my face,
Sniffing the marsh smells and lake smells
As I listen to the calls of unseen shorebirds.
And I'm glad as well to acknowledge my civic coordinates:
To be standing fifty yards from the Coast Guard station
Barely half a mile from downtown Buffalo,
At the western edge of the Empire State,
Which might have taken more care of its shoreline
Had it been ruled, now and then, by an emperor.

Self-seeding cottonwood that began to root
Some forty years back, I've read in a pamphlet,
After the beach shacks were torn down and dredges
Stopped dumping the sludge from the channel here.
Trees that like their feet to stay wet while I
Am thankful for the boardwalk path
Lifted a yard above the cattails.

Of the dozen birds named on the sign
Beside their outlines, I can barely claim to know one
By sight or sound. But that doesn't mean
I'm too old to learn. Already I can distinguish
Their calls from the traffic noise blowing in,
Now and then, from the Skyway, and the ship horns,
And the lunchtime bells from the Cathedral.

Maybe when I learn to listen, I'll hear
The tree toads scratching, or the tree roots
Gripping the stone-rich soil and drinking,
Or the termites tunneling in the logs—
All oblivious to how close they are

To what used to be numbered among the top three
Grain ports of the Western world.

So what if the grain is stored elsewhere now.
It's time to focus on the life at hand,
Which explains why I've donned my safari hat
And brought my binoculars:
Because it's now or never if I want to become
Familiar with the residents of my neighborhood,
Including these pioneer cottonwood
Rising above the boardwalk
And the birds unseen at rest in the canopy.

And why not include the three fellow pedestrians
Now approaching at a leisurely pace,
Who nod when I nod, as if they knew me
Or knew my kind. "Look, here's another
Late-blooming, cottonwood-loving creature
With a northerly range." Or, "Here's another
Self-appointed surveyor of urban wetlands
Who hopes to learn on the job
All he needs to know."

Fast Food

I'd like to believe that the middle-aged woman
Eating her dinner alone at the picnic table
Provided by Ernie's Red Hots, just off Route 5,
Between Woodlawn and Silver Creek,
Hasn't made a wrong turn in life that's deprived her
Of friends and family. I'd like to believe that the words
She was writing a moment ago weren't part of a letter
Accusing someone of betrayal or indifference
But were notes to herself, perhaps for an article
She's been asked to write by the magazine she works for
On fast-food providers on the eastern shore of Lake Erie.
Which of them take pride in their work—that's the question
She may have committed herself to investigate.
Here's a woman who's always found work in an office
Too confining, who loves exploring the hinterlands.
Thirty years ago she might have joined her brother
In the study of law if lawyers still rode circuits
As they did in the era of her father's granddad.
How sad to her the thought of being stuck forever
Inside one courthouse, though she'd like to believe
That some of the clerks at work in her brother's office
May find, as they browse a magazine on their break,
The very article she's now doing the research for
And be gladdened to learn they needn't be rich
To afford a meal that will leave them feeling
They've received, for once, far more than they expected.
The rolls at Ernie's, they'll learn, whether white
Or whole grain, are fresh, and the mustard
Offers an artful blend of piquant spices.
Before she gathers her notes and goes,
She may copy Ernie's address from her place mat
So she can send her review when it's published.

His own conviction of being true to his standards,
She realizes, may be all that matters. Still,
It's also true that a stranger's endorsement
May prove of use when he asks himself
If he's doing the work he was meant to do,
Or some of the work, at least, if not all.

Bad Days, Good Days

On good days as well as bad the odds
Against my birth seem overwhelming.
But on my bad days they imply that my claim
To existence is tenuous, barely more real
Than the claim of the billions of others
Who missed the cut, while on my good days
My presence seems like a miracle.

It hurts my pride on my bad days to recall
The story my mother told about her parents:
How they wouldn't have met if the train
That carried her father to the ship waiting at Hamburg
Hadn't broken down in a field near Brest-Litovsk
So he had to leave for America seven days later
On the ship that carried my grandma-to-be.

It hurts my pride to feel my destiny
Bound up with a broken axle or gasket,
But on my good days the wonder I feel
Is a smaller version of the wonder
Felt by cosmologists when they consider
How close the cosmos itself came to missing
The boat into being, to losing its chance
For passengers, ports, and oceans,
For stars as plentiful as grains of beach sand.

The difference between my wonder and theirs
Is that mine is infused, on my good days,
With gratitude. Of course, they're pleased
That everything managed to clamber aboard
In the nick of time, but the alternative,
Nothing at all, is too wispy for them to grasp,

Whereas for me the story of Grandpa's train
Grinding to a halt on a snowy plateau
Is a gift I never grow tired of opening.

What a privilege it is for me to join him
While he paces beside the track as night comes on.
What a privilege to share his brooding
On the difference between his life
If he makes his ship and his life if he doesn't.

On my bad days choice seems denied him.
He's no more free than the train is free to stop
Or start when it pleases, or to leave the track.
On my good days he's free to interpret the accident
As one last chance to cancel his plan to emigrate
And return to his friends and family, who want him to stay.
And now I conceive him as free to set the question
Aside awhile to note that the scene before him
Would merit a painter's close attention.

There he is, letting the lantern light absorb him
As it falls on the workmen kneeling in the shadows
Beside the engine while the snowy fields
Stretch away behind them into the framing dark.
And now above them a display of stars
Appears to be just in time, after a journey
Of many eons, to complete a picture
He isn't likely to see again.

Know Yourself

Know yourself, says the oracle at Delphi,
Confirming my doubts about oracles,
Their assumption the self is a book
Waiting for someone like me to read it,
Not a coat I stitch together each day
From dreams and wishes, habits and moods.

If you know, says the oracle, that the portion
Of courage you've been allotted is small,
Better avoid a career in fighting fires.
If you know that you're short on patience,
Think twice about a career in teaching.
But who's to say you couldn't acquire the courage

To enter a burning house if you served a long
Apprenticeship in dousing porch fires?
Who's to say you couldn't learn patience
By waiting a minute longer each day
For a student to follow the steps of your argument?
Not long ago I would fret when waiting in line

On the day of a concert to buy a ticket,
Thinking about the music I could be hearing
At home on the stereo, though I knew the concert
Might make me feel part of a ritual
That ushered beauty into the world.
But now I welcome the urge to join the audience.

Yesterday I would have felt extra lucky
To learn, when I reached the window,
That my ticket was the last one available.
But today I feel sorry that the woman behind me,

9

Who's been willing to chat with me
For close to an hour, will miss the music.

Am I really disturbed by the thought
She deserves to go far more than I do,
Having bought her ticket weeks back
Just to be sure she'd have one
Only to lose it yesterday evening
When she left her purse untended for just a moment?

Who will I be today, I wonder: a person willing
To right a wrong by offering her my ticket,
Or a person content with hoping she's found
Our talk so agreeable she's glad the last seat
Has gone to someone who seems a kindred spirit,
Not just to anyone?

Joseph's Work

He's done his work well for many decades,
Overseeing the produce at the market
His brothers own, where I've had a chance
To benefit from his careful diligence
In maintaining quality in the bins,
The same virtue displayed on a larger scale
By the Joseph his parents were thinking of
In naming him, the favorite son of Jacob,
Who ended up as the overseer
Of all the Egyptian granaries.

Like the brothers of Joseph in the Bible,
His brothers, he's implied in a few asides
Over the years, haven't behaved as brothers should,
Though they never threw him into a pit,
Angry their father loved him the most.
It was more a case of everyday bullying
That his father noticed but didn't stop.

As for forgiving them all as Jacob's son
Forgives his brothers—weeping with joy
When they come from Canaan in a time of famine
To buy grain—there the Joseph I know
Admits that he's fallen short,
Though he's tried to resist resentment
By avoiding their company evenings and weekends.

And now and then on Sunday, when the weather's good,
I've passed him as he's sat on a bench
In our local graveyard. Maybe it eases him
To wonder how many of the dead around him
Might have been happier if they'd managed

To put away thoughts of blame,
How many, if they couldn't manage to wish
Their brothers well, managed at least
Not to wish them ill.

And the next day he's back at work,
Making distinctions between plums
Fit to be served at a banquet and plums
Fit to be served at a potluck supper at home,
Marked by more than the usual lumps and bruises
But still to be savored, not too tart or sweet.

Blind Guest

I want to believe in him, the blind man
Who makes the other guests at the dinner table
Forget his blindness as he launches himself
Into the talk around him. I want to believe
He's moved by the lively exchange of opinions,
Not by the fear he won't be asked to dinner
Again if he sits all evening in silence
And the silence is read as suggesting
That luck alone has spared the others his hardship,
That by rights his days should be sunny too.

If I can believe he isn't looking for sympathy,
That he doesn't expect me to share his burden,
I'll feel so grateful that I may be willing
To do what I can to share it. Though I can't
Loan him my eyes once a week
For an hour or two, I can try to dwell
On the good it might do him to escape
The pervading dark for even a moment,
To visit the world only light reveals.

And I can try to picture how reluctant he'd be
To return the loan when the hour was out,
How unfair it would seem to him that I
Would be the lender always and he the borrower.

Two Lives

In my other life the B-17 my father is piloting
Is shot down over Normandy
And my mother raises her sons alone
On her widow's pension and on what she earns
As a nurse at the local hospital, a sum
That pays for a third-floor walk-up
In a neighborhood that's seen better days.
I play stickball after school in the lot
Behind the laundry. I come home bruised
From fistfights and snowball fights
With boys who live in the tenement on the corner.
Not once do I play with the boy I am
In this life, whose father, too old for the draft,
Starts a paint company in a rented basement
That almost goes under after a year
And then is saved, as the war continues,
By a steady flow of government contracts
That allows my mother to retire from nursing
And devote herself to work with the poor.
I find our quiet neighborhood of handsome houses
And shady streets crushingly uneventful.
No surprise I spend hours each day turning the pages
Of stories about trolls, wizards, giants,
Wandering knights, and captive princesses.
In my other life, I have to leave high school
To bolster the family income as lab boy
In the building attached to the factory that in this life
My father owns. I clean test tubes and beakers,
With a break for stacking cans on the loading dock
Or driving the truck to make deliveries.
In this life it takes only one summer of work
At my father's office, addressing announcements

Of a coating tougher than any made by competitors,
To decide that the real world, so called,
Is overrated, compared to the world of novels,
Where every incident is freighted with implications
For distinguishing apparent success from actual.
No wonder I'm leaning toward a profession
Where people can earn a living by talking
In class about books they love. Meanwhile,
In my other life, after helping to bring the union
To a non-union shop, I rise in the ranks
To become shop steward, and then,
Helped by a union scholarship,
I earn a degree in labor law.
I bring home casebooks on weekends
To the very block where I happen to live
Ensconced in this life, here in a gray-green house
With dark-brown trim. If I don't answer the bell
On weekends in summer, I'm in the garden,
Strolling the shady path beneath the maples,
Musing on the difference between a life
Deficient in incident and a life uncluttered.
Seated at my patio table, I write a letter
Asking a friend what book has he read
In the last few months that has opened his eyes
On a subject that's likely to interest me.
Meanwhile, across the street, in the garden
Of my other life, I can often be found
Hoeing the rutabaga and beans and cabbage
I plan to share with neighbors in the hope they're moved
To consider planting a garden where many
May do the weeding together, and the watering.
It won't be long till I knock at the door of the house

Where in this life I'm at my desk preparing a class
On solitude in the novels of the Romantics.
Do I say to myself it's one more stranger
Eager to sell me something or make a convert,
Or do I go down to see who's there?

In the Woods

It seems like a prayer modest enough
To be answered: to enjoy my usual
Two-week stay at the rented cabin
Deep in the woods, to fend off the loneliness
That pushed in last summer from nowhere
After a day or two.

A prayer to savor the solitude once again,
To regard the cabin not as forlorn
But as expectant. One of its favorite guests
Has returned to resume the first-day rituals
That both delight in: wiping the dust
From the wicker furniture, mopping the pine floor,
Cutting the weeds back that crowd the porch.

A prayer that the trail from the yard to the lake
Will seem to welcome me back with the question,
Where have you been hiding yourself,
You and your hickory walking stick,
Your floppy sun hat and purple beach towel?

Only a matter of minutes then,
If my prayer is answered,
Before I'm moved to approach the rowboat
Lying facedown in the uncut grass,
Dreaming of coves and inlets
It used to visit.

Then to break the spell by heaving it over
While uttering words of encouragement:
Wake up, my boat. The coves and inlets
I'll row you to may look at first

Like many others. But then
You'll recognize where you are.

To Earth

If you're a god, as some believe,
You're one of the few not made in the image of man,
For you have no ears to hear our many petitions,
No eyes to watch how we bow our heads.
And yet your skin of grasses, leaves, and petals
Flutters when touched by the faintest eddy of air.

A god without legs for striding off when displeased,
Without hands for snatching your gifts from our hands
When we don't deserve them. And still you offer
A bounty you haven't promised to give,
And not merely to us but to the crows
Making a hubbub in a dead magnolia,
To the swallows nesting in a garage.

No head for nodding to confirm a solemn edict.
No shoulders to shrug in dismissing the doings
Of creatures that we shrug off as beneath our notice.
For you the poise that a cloud of midges
Displays in floating above a hedge.
For you its deftness at moving off
All at once at a signal too faint
For our antennae to pick up.

An Actress

I have to admire my neighbor across the street
For deciding to be insincere
Where I'm concerned, now that she recognizes
She sincerely dislikes our chance encounters
For reasons that she's not proud of: my heavy brow
That seems a duplicate of the brow
Of a bully at work; my lantern jaw
That mirrors the jaw of the manager at her bank
Who denied her a loan she'd counted on.

To serve the cause of fairness, she must be a pharisee,
Making a show of interest she doesn't feel,
Waving and smiling, even crossing the street
To ask what I've been up to this spring,
Like somebody not indifferent to my answers.

If she goes through the motions, she reasons,
She may take the first step on the road to change.
Her inner self, noticing that her outer self
Is making an effort to be neighborly,
Will be shamed by how dull her performance is,
How spiritless, how wooden.

To make it convincing, she has to imagine
What someone might feel who meant
Every gesture she made as gospel.
The more she practices, the easier it becomes,
Or should become. And if it doesn't, too bad.
The show must go on, graceful or awkward,
A pleasure to be a part of, or a chore.

My Defender

What I need at the moment, besides more luck
In making my life eventful, is a defender,
Someone who regards any comment of mine
That seems to betoken a grudging spirit
As misleading, as failing to express
My deep convictions.

If I suggest, when we walk along the jetty
Not far from my house, that the fisherman
Casting all morning in a rowboat among the reeds
Without one strike is an image of life—
A long wait for what never happens—
My defender will tell me I mean to say
I hope the man catches a fish by nightfall.

If I compare a cloud to a bruise
On the face of a fighter who's almost ready
To throw in the towel, my defender will argue
I mean that after another day of rain
The sky may be able to heal itself.

Deeper than the history of my opinions
Lies the history of my wishes,
Which my defender will have studied carefully,
While no one else will have even skimmed it,
Not even me.

How good it will be, when we visit
The jetty in winter, to hear that it isn't like me
To refer to the few birds left—now flying
In circles above the icy water
And now alighting—as malingerers,

Too faint of heart or too lazy
For the long flight south.

What I really mean, declares my defender,
Is that I admire their courage
For daring to stay when pickings are slim
Here where the green world has succumbed to snow.

II

Table

Once I could move this table of solid teak
From the basement to the patio by myself.
Now to perform this April ritual
I need a friend to help me.
Still, I don't want to waste an afternoon
Lamenting the obvious: that the table
Dwells with the rest of my goods in the realm
Of space primarily, while I, along with other
Animate creatures, dwell primarily in time.
That wouldn't be fair to the table in question,
To reduce its purpose to mere resistance
To my diminishing muscle mass,
A table that freely offers its raised, flat surface
When I pull up a chair to write a list
Of the items I'll need for the supper I'm planning
To serve outside next Sunday, if the weather holds.
And why not prepare a question or two
To pose if the talk starts to drift toward lamenting
The obvious fact that the number of evenings left us
For talking around the table is dwindling.
What about asking for help with a question
About the music committee I've recently joined:
Why the churchgoing members seem content
With its slow progress in providing a school
Meagerly funded with a music program
While the nonbelievers seem disappointed?
Fine with me if my guests find this question
Less engaging than I do and turn to another,
Like whether music is merely an accident
In the evolution of humans or an active cause
In the long-term survival of our species.
And somebody else may ask the name

Of the bird that's singing that very minute
High in the canopy of the linden tree.
It isn't likely they'll come to any conclusion
By the time they leave, but that doesn't mean
They'll regard the talk at the table as wasted,
This table that a friend has promised to help me
Move to the basement when the trees are bare.

A Proposal

Why don't we set aside for a day
Our search for variety and have lunch
At the same café where we had lunch yesterday
And order the same avocado and Gouda sandwich
On whole wheat bread, toasted and buttered?

Why don't we stroll again after lunch
To the river and back? I'll be glad to interpret
Your wearing the blouse you wore yesterday
As a sign you're still the person I think you are,
That this is the walk you want to take,

The one you didn't get your fill of before.
And later, why don't we hope for a sunset
That duplicates the valiant effort of yesterday:
Enough clouds for the light to play with,
Despite a haze that dims the hues?

Isn't the insight worth repeating
That the end of the day may show itself
To be just as colorful as the beginning,
That a fine beginning isn't a veil
That the end is destined to strip away?

The same words, but yesterday
They may have sounded a little tentative,
As if we weren't sure we were ready
To stand behind them. Now if we choose
To repeat them, it means we are.

Clippers

I know I borrowed these clippers I'm using
To trim this boxwood border
And believe the lender was a man my age.
It's just that I can't recall his name now
Or how long ago exactly I borrowed them.

Why he hasn't dropped by to claim them
Now that it's spring again is another question.
If he thinks I've kept them too long,
He should give me a chance to prove that what seems
To him a failure of courtesy isn't intentional.

If he's forgotten the name of the man
He loaned them to and is willing to speculate
On whether we share this problem,
We should hit it off if we ever meet.

I'll mean it when I thank him for making a loan
That turned out longer than I expected.
He'll mean it when he thanks me
For keeping his clippers in good condition,
Sharpened and oiled.

Then, if he asks me, I may share with him
My philosophy of trimming, or at least the part
I've carried with me into the present:
How I'm not concerned with showing the bushes
Who's boss by cutting them down to size,
Just with making the path look cared for
And the porch inviting.

Then, if I ask him, he may share with me
Some of the tactics he uses to counter
The slippage of names from his memory,
The exercises he's found that stir his spirits.

Try to guess, I can hear him saying,
Whether the wind now ruffling the boxwood
Is bringing a fragrance from woodlands
You visited often in times gone by
Or whether you never glimpsed them
But have no trouble believing
That if you had, you would have enjoyed them.

It doesn't matter which, I hear him saying,
So long as you recognize the day as ideal
For working outside. Devote yourself to the trimming.
Don't feel obliged to ask if this is the first time
You'll be giving the ritual your full attention.
Don't waste time wondering if it's the last.

Power

It's a good thing that man is a god in ruins,
As Emerson calls him, not a god in his prime,
Considering that just yesterday,
When a driver cut into my lane on the Thruway
To make the turnoff—forcing me into a skid
That flung my bag of groceries to the floor—
My wish for revenge, had it been backed
By a godlike capacity, might have resulted
In his car's crashing against a guardrail
And flipping over into the river below.
So this morning I'd be starting my first full day
As a murderer. Instead, with my anger
Already a night behind me—my hot-faced,
Fist-shaking outrage—I can be glad for once
Not only that I'm not a god but that no god
Is willing to do my bidding, and no cohort
Of fellow humans. What a blessing
If no one at all was listening.
Now to be thankful for my obscurity.
Now to begin to enjoy sharing the road
With a colorful medley of drivers
On various missions I must learn to distinguish
If I want to appreciate the world I live in.
How sad to dwell in the dark of yesterday
With a man who can only divide the multitude
Into drivers who stay in their lanes
And drivers who don't. On one side, the many
Smart ones careful not to intrude
On his agenda; on the other, the fool or two
Reckless enough to try.

A Friend and a Book

I bring a book when I go to meet, for coffee,
My great-hearted friend Louisa, who does all she can
To help when I need a favor, and does it
Not from a sense of obligation that others
May have to fall back on, but because it makes her happy
To smooth my way. I bring a book because her heart
Has room for others as well as for me,
And not only for other friends but for strangers
Not on her schedule when she sets out on a day
Like this one to meet me for coffee at 5:15
At the outdoor café only a five-minute walk
From the hospital where she works in admissions.
Five minutes unless she spies a man on the corner
Who looks confused as he compares the street names
With names on the slip of paper he's holding.
She can't walk by without first pausing to offer
What information she has. And if she can't understand
His accent, and can't make clear her directions
To the street named on the slip he hands her,
What else can she do but make a detour?
Meanwhile, at the café, I'm reading a book of poems
I only leafed through before, just long enough to make clear
It was worth going back to when I had more time.
Now I may have time to mark all the poems
I wish I'd written, and then to push past the endless
Fret about competition to the pleasure of finding
I live in an era where real achievement is possible.
By the time Louisa finally arrives,
I may have a list of poems I want to read her.
But first I'll ask for the story of her adventures
In the realm of extra sympathy that I myself

Don't feel obliged to dwell in, though I feel obliged
To show I'm thankful to those who do.

A History of Nagging

Maybe the nagging of your little boy to stop,
On the way home from the zoo, at a toy store
Or an ice-cream stand isn't an effort
To pay you back for your nagging him
To sit up straight or straighten his room.
He may be trying to practice resisting authority
While obeying, a skill that later he may find a use for
Beyond the simple thrill of self-assertion.
Instead of treating it as a habit to break,
Think of it as essential to who he is,
As if it were present before birth
In his spirit's longing to return to earth.
Other shades may have been reluctant to bear
Again the weight of the body, but his shade
Nagged the attendants to let it go back at once.
This time it would fight for the general welfare
Against the powerful. Of course, it forgot
Much of its pledge after the requisite sip
From the cup of oblivion. Still your boy's nagging
To go to camp may imply not merely the wish
To escape your authority but the wish to engage
At last with a world that won't withhold
What it has to offer if he's persistent.
Don't be surprised if he nags his counselor
To let him go on an overnight with the older boys
And fall asleep on a blanket under the stars.
Don't be put out, after he's worked as a counselor
Himself for seven summers, if he wants to bring back
From the woods a gospel of woodland quiet.
A life of teaching may seem to him then an adventure
If he can persuade a fellow counselor,
His fetching friend Maria, that they're more than friends,

That they're meant to be a couple, which means,
When she hesitates, he'll insist on making
His case to her for an hour each evening.
Your task as father isn't to interfere
But to caution him that he runs the risk
Of making himself a bore with his nagging insistence
That destiny backs their union as much as he does.
This is your chance to suggest he set repetition
Aside awhile and try a single extravagant gesture
Like sending her a check for a million dollars
With a note suggesting that she wait awhile to cash it,
That in the meantime whatever he has is hers.

In the Moment

If, in her next letter, she counsels me
To live in the moment, I'll be glad to try
So long as she doesn't expect me
To set aside as mere distraction
All the wishes the moment can't satisfy.

I'm willing, for instance, to be more attentive
On my walks alone to the river and back
If she thinks I should be, so long
As it's understood she'll be glad to read
Any comments about them I want to send,
Which seems to suggest that the moment
Needs more than itself to be complete.

And if, when she visits, instead of walking
Down to the beach, she prefers to sit on the porch
And talk about why her job in public relations
At a resort hotel doesn't fulfill her wish
To serve the public, I won't use her advice
Against her, won't recommend
That she try to be more accepting.

I'll do my best to listen with sympathy
And make suggestions about other work
Available now that she might like more.
And while I do, I may speculate to myself
About work not available that might suit her best.

It's easy for me to picture her as a scout
On a wagon train, skilled in riding ahead
To choose a campsite, admired for her prudence

Whereas others, impatient to reach the end,
Are liable to push their luck.

For her to live in the moment then
Doesn't mean believing the site she's chosen
Is perfect. I can hear her admitting
She wishes it lay nearer a woods,
With fuel at hand for the cooking fires,
Though she's glad there's a brook nearby
And an ample patch of grass for the oxen.

As for the river they've been hoping to cross,
There isn't time now to reach it by sundown.
Tomorrow she can help them find a spot
Where the banks are less steep and rocky,
The water more shallow and more slow.

Not Description

Often a sentence that's true,
Like "The window is closed," is less interesting
Than a sentence neither true nor false,
Like "Let's open the window
So the air of April can enter the room,"
A proposal that doesn't describe what is the case
So much as nudge it in a new direction.

And if then you add, "Trust me to close it
If you find the air too chilly," you'll be doing more
Than describing what you are likely to do.
You'll be bringing something new into the present,
A promise that remains in force
Whatever the weather, whatever your mood.

"Come to the window and see how the snow
Has melted, how umber buds stipple the branches,"
Is less a description than an invitation.
And if the invited one is reluctant,
It's time for a sentence that appeals to hope
Far more than to memory:

"May this spring be the one we're looking for;
May whatever kept us before
From preparing a proper welcome
Not keep us now."

A Letter

I hope you're glad I'd rather send you
A letter by regular mail than a message
Beamed in an instant from screen to screen.
To fold the pages twice and insert them
Into an envelope seems to make them
More of a gift, to wrap them, to suggest
I've chosen my words for you alone,
The very person whose name I've written
In longhand on the envelope I'll carry
To the mailbox at the corner tomorrow morning,
Braving the cold for the early pickup.
I hope you consider the stamp part of the gift,
Not a flag to suggest I back my country
Whatever it does, but the silhouette of a bird
That doubtless appears at your feeder often,
Now that winter is here in earnest.
First-class postage, expressing a faith
I hope you share: that the statements enclosed
Will prove as true three days from now
As they are this moment, that they represent
Firm convictions, not passing fancies.
And think of the faith my letter expresses
That the world can be relied on to help us,
That others will do their part to move
The letter forward to your address:
Letter gatherers and letter sorters,
Mailbag loaders at the airport, pilots to fly it
Over lakes and mountains while the nation below
Goes about its business or lies asleep,
Till the letter rests in the box on your porch.
And because it's a gift, not required by duty
Or courtesy, you can take its sentences

To mean what they seem to mean, expressing
The thoughts of the person I really am
Or at least of the person I may become
If I keep practicing, day by day.

A Typescript

The book on ending war once and for all
That my friend devoted the last ten years
Of his life to finishing still sits on my shelf
In typescript, though I promised him,
In an effort to ease his final hours,
To do my best to find a publisher.

A book that's argued as forcefully as any
Can be when based on the shaky premise
That most people have good intentions,
That they're as open as he was to supposing
Countries, like individuals, can learn to agree
On simple rules promoting the general welfare
And obey them gladly even when inconvenient.

If the trillions of cells we're each composed of,
His argument goes, manage to work together
Without a leader or contract, it's possible
That the far fewer creatures of thought like us
Can reach consensus if we keep talking.

His mistake is the mistake of genius,
If Emerson's definition of *genius* is accurate:
"To believe . . . what is true for you in your private heart
Is true for all men," a belief he supports
With examples showing how people often
Sell themselves short, how they assume
Their moments of generous impulse
To be less significant than they really are.

The only editor willing to give me an interview
Told me the book had no target audience

Waiting to read it, that an audience
Had to be found, not made.

The audience in the office consisted of two:
A friend of the late author and an editor
Not willing to edit the book in question,
Each composed of trillions of cells in harmony.
Two plus the fleshless ghost of my friend
Standing beside a bookcase crowded with books
Far less substantial than his typescript,
Nodding in silence to urge me on.

At the Graveyard

Now they don't need a thing from us,
However small: not even a cup of water
Scooped from the fountain; not even a slight
Adjustment of leg or shoulder
To ease a cramp, or an offer to read them
A poem or two they used to like.

And now they have nothing to offer us,
Poor wanderers without luggage,
Without maps or pockets.
No blessings, no answers to any questions
We can think of asking, no words of advice
Besides the words that we choose to lend them.

Nothing to give us now or receive, and yet
Here we are with our bright bouquets
As if to say we still remember the light
Lost when they left us, and the light
They bestowed on us that we can't repay.

Emily's Birthday

It isn't likely to transform your life,
Your desire to buy a birthday gift for Emily,
But it may transform an empty hour
Into a full one. It may remind you
That the bookstore you've often browsed in
Is more than the halfway marker
On the way home from the clinic
That it seemed reduced to yesterday,
The day of your yearly checkup.
It's a place to search for a gift on a subject
That seldom fails to engage her, like plant ecology
Or the habits of social animals.

The errand won't counter your worry
That fewer years are left you than you would like,
But it may assist you in setting that worry aside
For a while as you give yourself
To making the best selection.

You won't know the title until you find it,
But you know already it won't be a screed
That argues the earth is a hopeless case.
Better a book on protecting the habitat
Of beleaguered species, on transforming
Eroded fields into woods or meadows.

And if the clerk at the gift-wrap counter
Looks gaunt as a ghost, as you imagine
The Angel of Death might look
When announcing it's time to ask
If your life has been meaningful, and if not,
Why not, the question will have to wait

Till you make it clear that the green paper
Is more appropriate than the charcoal,
And a ribbon not pink or white
But the bright yellow of forsythia.

III

On the Beach

This crowd of sunbathers on the beach
Shows that the feel of sun on the skin
Helps foster peace in a time of contention.
Just look at us all, how each is content for now
With a plot of land no bigger than a beach towel,
At rest among strangers who seem familiar
In the pleasure they take in receiving the light,
A gift that's come a long way to reach them.

Strangers just inches apart, but not one of us
Considers digging a moat and posting a guard
Even when the book we've brought along
Falls from our hands and we feel ourselves
Drifting toward sleep to the steady beat
Of the waves breaking and falling back.

So many content to dream of sun and sand,
So few compelled to dream of rowing alone
To an island far out in the bay where a hermit
Waits with a map to a tower that holds a princess
Languishing with her father, the rightful king.

And then the voice of somebody softly muttering
Intrudes on your doze, someone you find,
When you look around, to be a woman
Just a towel away, rummaging in her beach bag,
Vexed with herself for forgetting her tanning oil.

Should you point out that the sun has nearly
Dropped too low in the sky to burn?
No. You understand, as you offer her yours,
That she wants the sun to stay where it is

Till it's etched in her memory, a reminder
That the world of discord she'll soon return to
Will be claiming too much
When it claims it's the only world.

Crosstown Bus

Between an ad for healthier skin
And an ad for a night-school program
In business management, a narrow panel
Filled by four words: "Live all you can."
No phone number provided, no address,
So it isn't likely sponsored by a travel bureau
Or a real estate office. Maybe a church
That chooses for now to remain anonymous
Is eager to share its one commandment
So we don't decide to postpone our lives
Till our skin is healthier or till a business degree
Hangs in our office. Live all you can,
Just as you are. Don't hold back while you wait
For a vision to show you the best path forward.
Don't wait for a society more congenial.
Trust the one you're offered on this very bus.
Yes, your information is limited.
Yes, it seems that the young man in front,
Standing up to offer his seat to the man with a cane,
Is practicing courtesy, but is that enough
To indicate that he's living all he can?
And what about the old woman across the aisle
Asleep in the window seat, with her purse unguarded
On the seat beside her, and her velvet coat?
Hard to say if she needs a lecture on caution
Or if she has joined the fabled few
Who regard possessions as shells
Washing up on the beach each morning,
Meant to be given away by nightfall.
And if she's attached to her purse and coat,
Does she suppose that the trust required
For believing she needn't worry about them

Will soon be hers if she behaves
As if it's hers already? I trust you,
She may be saying to the other riders,
So why not begin to trust yourselves?

To the People of 2060

It's not as if we never consider you,
Never suppose that unless we do something drastic
We'll be leaving you a spoiled version
Of the planet we received in fair condition.

Still, your troubles feel far off, while ours
Press in on us, including our ailing parents,
Balky children, and friends we can see now
Only by turning the pages of an album.

If you could send us a photo that shows
The street we live on flooded by glacier melt,
Or a meadow we like to visit
Scorched by the sun, we might be moved
To intervene so emphatically
That the image would prove too dark an omen.

Don't put it off. We need your evidence now
So we don't regard the health of the biosphere
As a problem we're free to pass on,
As those who tried to secure our liberty
By crafting the Constitution
Passed slavery on to be dealt with
By an era they hoped more enlightened than theirs.

A hundred years after the slaves were freed
Believers in freedom rode buses south
To help the bravest among the unregistered
Walk to the courthouse. But help for you
In a hundred years will arrive too late.

Can you beam us a signal that we can read
Showing a future that's all too likely
Unless we devote ourselves to an alternative
Far less likely but not impossible?

If not, can you send us at least a postcard
Announcing you'll soon be packing your bags
And giving your movers our address?
A card in your own clear hand to convince us
You're not a ghostly abstraction but flesh and blood
About to set out for the homestead
We've been assigned to prepare for your arrival.

A card that prompts us to do enough
So we're sorry we won't be here
To greet you in person, not relieved.

Favorite God

Not the omnipotent one, who works alone,
But the one who finds the job of keeping the world
Running peaceably too much for him
And is grateful for help from other gods,
And doesn't mind if they receive all the credit.

The one uneasy when any prayers of thanks
Are wafted his way, any smoke of sacrifice.
Let farmers show their gratitude for the rain
By thanking the god of rain directly.
Let a district delivered from a plague of locusts
Sing hymns to the god of early frost.

As for the prayers of those who seek protection
From acts of injustice, each is a thorn
In the flesh of the god in question,
Who knows how little relief he can bring.

Little relief for the prisoner
Unwilling to join a gang, when he tries
To make it safely across the yard.
Little relief for the seamstress on the factory floor
Who resembles too closely the wife of the foreman,
Who ran off last week with a younger man.

Yes, this god has been known to soften
The hardest hearts when given the months
Or years the process requires. But what about
Having to act at once in emergencies?

No time to explain to the bully
The source of his need to cross the street

And mock the boy whose ears stick out.
No time to convince the boy his humiliation
Will allow him one day to be more compassionate.

No wonder this favorite god is ready to deal
With any god who might offer a sudden
Evasive maneuver, this bargaining god
Who isn't worried about his dignity.

I can see him now, promising the god of geese
He'll do what he can to shorten the hunting season
Or protect more wetlands if a flock
Can sweep down Court Street in the next two minutes,
Skimming so low that in the surprise and confusion
The boy in danger might slip away.

A Traveler from Altruria

Just like your country, my country
Doesn't have enough beds for everyone,
Enough bedrooms, closets, porches, and yards.
But in my country we address the problem
By customs obliging those who possess these items
To loan them, without any charges,
Two days a week to those who don't.

A clear gain for the borrowers:
To feel that having enough isn't a dream
That might come true one day for their children
But an actual fact for themselves every weekend.
Meanwhile, the lenders gain by learning
From their two-day stint in tents or barracks
How lucky they are to have so much
Waiting for them when they get home.

And when the lenders find that their stoves
Need to be cleaned more often, they're glad
To imagine the ample meals
Their visitors must have enjoyed in their kitchens.
And if they discover grass stains
On the tablecloth in the dining room,
They're pleased to think that their yard
Inspired their visitors to enjoy a picnic.

And if the margins of some of their books
Are filled with notes in a strange hand,
They're glad to compare the new notes with the old,
Entering into a dialogue that may free their thought

From the thrall of habit and lead to insights
They couldn't have come to on their own.

And twice a year on the solstice our customs ordain
A potluck banquet where lenders and borrowers—
After serving each other their specialties—
Raise the question whether their customs
Are as good as can be expected
Or a stop on the road to something more.

When

He agrees that telling the truth is to be preferred
To lying, but the hard question is when to tell.
When does he tell the firm that's advertised
For an opening in their bookkeeping department
That he spent the last three years of his life
In prison for embezzlement? On the application,
In the box marked "prior experience,"
Or after they call him in for a second interview,
Or after ten years when he's worked his way up
To be vice president? It's a lie to hide it, he agrees,
But it only mirrors their lie that an honest answer
Won't reduce his chances of being hired to zero.
The important truth is the one he can't prove:
That he's determined not to repeat his crime
Here in a country famous for second chances.
He loves the truth, but haven't the people
Who'll conduct the interview ever hidden
Part of the truth when they applied for an opening?
Chances are that a few were silent about being fired
From a prior job in sales for making promises
That stretched the fabric of truthfulness till it tore.
Chances are that a few, when asked to go into detail
On their theory of marketing, withheld the truth
Of their long flirtation with the doctrine that bluffing
Had built the country, the brag of brochures
That depicted a swamp in the wilderness as a bustling town.
They want to forget their past, but he is resolved
To remember his and so be more forgiving
When he's responsible for enforcing the rules.
Any new hires of his that cross the line
Between operating within the law and just outside it
Will be given a warning. And then, if they're fired,

He won't take them to court unless he's sure
The judge will err on the side of clemency. Not three years
Behind bars but one year of community service,
Including helping out at the library
With processing all the books that turn up
By the carload during Forgiveness Week
When decades of fines are set aside.

Doe

Wary at the edge of the woods, the doe
Browses near dusk, in silence, head down
For just a moment, then glances up
To sniff the air, to listen.

Shy is the obvious adjective
To suggest its uncertain, tentative presence,
But *fearful* might be more accurate,
The open meadow more dangerous
Than the dim woods, though the woods too
Require more than a little vigilance.

Poised and watchful, alive in the moment,
Living the vivid life of the senses
That would crush me after five minutes
If I couldn't retreat from it when I wished
To the sanctum of my own thoughts,
Behind the door no one can open
Unless I want company.

How naked the doe appears to me,
How defenseless as she risks exposure
To feed a little, here in the twilight,
In a district of woods and meadows
That's losing ground to the steady spread
Of the district I have to acknowledge mine.

For the moment I'm glad the doe appears to count me
As one of the presences whose company isn't menacing
So long as I'm quiet and keep my distance.
And then I'm glad she's startled by something
I'm not aware of and darts away.

Nothing

Nothing is more annoying than a stranger in town
Standing forlorn in front of a modest hotel
He's just been told that he can't afford,
Who seems to be hoping some driver like me,
Moved by his plight, will pull to the curb
And offer a home-cooked dinner and a guest room.
Where does he think he is, in a town
That obeys the rules of hospitality
Passed down unbroken from some golden age?
If his parents thought they were doing their son
A favor by withholding the real name
Of the age he lived in, they were mistaken.

The only thing more annoying is a stranger
Who expects too little, who believes he's lucky—
After spending a day in town looking for work,
And failing—if no one tells him to move along.
A man who's delighted, after finding no room
At the inn for the likes of him, to find behind it
A field just right for resting. Where is the anger
He ought to be feeling at that moment?
And then I have to put up with his joy
At being allowed to watch the slow
Procession of stars across the sky
Without having to buy a ticket.

Wallace Siner

Years later, I learned from a site on the Web
He was thirty, a captain, when he was killed
By small-arms fire, "leaving behind
A wife and two sons." But then,
Besides the fact that he died in Vietnam,
All I knew about him was the name
Handed to me on an otherwise blank card
Just before the long line I was moving in
Finally passed the front gate of the White House
And I took my turn at shouting my two-word speech
Into the dark night of November 15, 1969.
Too bad the president wasn't at home,
That he missed the fiery speeches delivered all day
That I can't recall now, and the candlelight procession
I recall only one moment of, the moment
I flung the name through the fence, a stone
I couldn't hear landing, though it seemed then
An accusation far more substantial
Than any insult I might have shouted
Or any statement of principle. Two words
With some grit of personal essence still clinging.
Of course, I knew I couldn't say them
As his parents had, or any brothers or sisters,
Or the buddies in his platoon, or his high school classmates,
Or even the second cousins he may have met once a year
At a family reunion. No way for me
To know back then if he believed in the war
Or if, while hating it, he felt obliged as a citizen
To go where the government that the people had chosen
Chose to send him. It seems odd I never forgot
The name of someone I never met, while forgetting
The names of many who cared about me,

Who backed me up when I needed backing.
I wish I could say their names today
And the saying could make their presence,
Dim to me now, more vivid. Still I'm grateful
I can remember the name of someone who died
In a war I was lucky enough to miss. Back then,
Fifty years ago, I shouted it as a challenge.
Now, as I wonder how much of whoever I was
Still lives, I say it quietly to myself.

Tents and Houses

To live in the world as the Hebrews lived in the desert,
In tents, not houses—that was the advice that Augustine
Gave his congregation when the eternal order
Established by Rome was cracking and crumbling.
Put your trust, he urged, in a promised land
Beyond the tremors and rockslides of history.

It took a long while for a promised land on earth
As well as heaven to seem possible once again.
If not here, then elsewhere. If not in the old world,
Then with the Pilgrims, say, in the new. It was time
For the venturous few to cross the wilderness
Of the ocean and build on a hill a city closer
In spirit to the lofty original than any before.

And if, after a few generations, their achievement
Proved less inspiring than expected, if the city
Resembled too closely those left behind,
Still, houses of worship of many kinds,
On every corner, preached to their congregations
On the need for reform, and many listened.

And among the grown children who chose to move on,
Some dreamed of building a town more enlightened,
Though most journeyed west with their parents' blessings
Simply to look for land less crowded,
For soil less thin and rocky.

When they reached a likely spot for a farm
They dwelled in tents and lean-tos only as long
As it took them to build houses of logs and thatching,
Of brick and stone. Later the pitching of tents

Was left to the children on balmy evenings
When their parents let them sleep in the yard.

Soon the Sabbath became the day for a call
From a child in California with news
Of her new house on a hill near the ocean,
A day for hoping that those not settled
Be settled soon, that those still restless
Leave off their wandering in the wilderness
And make their way home with stories enough
In their duffel bags to last a lifetime.

And if a few of them feel the need
Now and then, on weekends, to distance themselves
From weekday habits, they may find relief
In a wooded campground a few miles off.
There they can leave their cars in the lot
And hike a mile to pitch their pup tents
And hang their provisions from a branch high up.

And after a day of swimming and climbing,
Of gathering wood for a cooking fire,
They may choose to sing, as the fire burns down,
A song of the road where the need to move on
Is more than matched by the traveler's recognition
He's homesick. He hears you calling, Shenandoah,
Though he's bound away, bound far away,
Across the wide Missouri.

Hunters

If my father had been a hunter
And had taught me to think of gun lore
As a part of wood lore, I might not regard
All hunters as killers, even if hunting had proved
For me, after a season or two,
A joyless pastime: transforming a deer
Bounding across a clearing or pausing
To catch a sound or a scent, into a carcass.

I might have been persuaded
He was doing the deer a service
By thinning the herd so it didn't starve
When the snow lay deep. I might have admired
His efforts at circulating petitions
To protect the woods from encroachment
By a new suburb or a larger mall.

A modest, thoughtful hunter like him
Wouldn't have driven through town with a dead deer
Draped on the hood to proclaim his prowess
As an angel of death to the herds, if not as a god.

Maybe he would have agreed if I'd argued
It takes a gifted and practiced woodsman
To leave his gun behind and follow the deer
Undetected on their retreat
Into the underbrush, like a reporter
Sent to investigate a local, reclusive tribe.

Big news from the woods in the first installment
Of a ten-part series that not one deer
Appears unhappy to be a deer.

Not one would prefer to be a bear or a cougar.
Not one is sorry it's not a man.

Evening with Washington

This evening I feel indebted to the snow
That's fallen all day in Washington Park
And is falling now, how it's softened
The statue of Washington on horseback
High on the knoll I've passed many evenings
Without much notice. What seemed before
A monument to a generic general
Seems now to present a man who knows
The odds are against him as he rides off
To answer his country's call, leaving behind
The only life he's used to and loves:
That of a planter in Virginia. Farewell
Maybe for many years to the gentleman
Content with improving the yield of his fields
Or adding to his ten thousand acres on the Potomac
Thirty thousand more in the valley of the Ohio.
Snow on his hat and shoulders, snow on the mane
And flanks of the bronze horse as the rider
Gives himself to keeping his ragtag band
Of Continentals from starving on rushed retreats,
From sleeping on frozen ground without a blanket.
I can't imagine stopping the life I've chosen
And starting another if told that a country
That didn't exist yet needed my services.
But at least I can change my perspective of him
Enough to acknowledge how much more
He opened himself to change than I do.
At least I can manage it now that the snow has offered
The cue I didn't know I needed. Will I forget,
By the time the snow has melted, what I'm feeling now?
I hope not, just as I hope that Washington,
When tending his fields many years afterward,

Didn't think of his time as general as a dream.
The titles that limit him to a single calling—
"Planter," "General," "President"—leave out too much,
And those that refer to many—"Father of his country,"
"First in the hearts of his countrymen"—sound vague.
Even the label "Slaveholder all his life,"
However true to the facts, seems inadequate,
Though he was zealous in the pursuit of runaways.
Now he's the product of his class and times;
Now he's the penitent who declares in his will
That when he dies his servants no longer
Will be his property, that they'll own themselves,
Free to become, if circumstances allow them,
One of the many persons each wants to be,
One if not more.

IV

Finding Thoreau

To visit the pond he ranked above all others
Is to be reminded that love sees
What it wants to see.
But to turn again to his book is to be persuaded
His loyalty was rewarded with a revelation
Not granted to those who come for a day.

To his neighbors he was a local eccentric
With little good to say about anyone.
To his readers he's a discoverer of a country
He's willing to share with them if they're willing
To say goodbye for a while to the country
They're used to and travel for many days.
They too can bathe in its waters each morning.
They too can sit on its shore all afternoon
Refining the gospel that less is more,
That solitude, rightly considered, is the best society.

As a place to visit, it's a Sunday outing.
As a place to read of, we can arrive—
After we cross a no-man's-land—
On a day that offers itself as a candidate
For a timeless Sabbath, the perfect occasion
To go exploring for something no more ethereal
Than a patch of huckleberries, no more mysterious.
Trust me, he says, and you won't regret it.
I'll be your guide to the spot
Where the earliest are sunning themselves
This very moment at a meadow's margin,
Waiting for you to pluck and eat.

Mrs. Gottlieb's Course in
World Literature

Few of us, she announced early on,
Were likely to have a guardian spirit devoted
To guiding us to the promised path, the one that led
To our becoming the person we were meant to be.
So if the advice of our parents and teachers
Didn't seem relevant, we'd be wise to turn
To the very books we'd be reading that semester:
Great novels and plays and poems, all starring
Versions of ourselves in situations akin
To those we'd be facing sooner than we supposed.
It wasn't too early for the girls to select
For their outside reading *Anna Karenina.*
Better find out at once how choosing passion
Above all else can sometimes leave us
Hemmed in more tightly than we were before.
As for the boys, those with a yen for detective fiction
Could write their papers on *Crime and Punishment.*
Time to move beyond asking who's the culprit
And consider what makes a crime a crime
And who is the proper judge of penitence.
So many questions to be raised and answered,
So many big decisions easy to miss
When they come disguised as small ones.
And life, she insisted, had already begun for us
Without fanfare, in earnest, at school, at home.
No way to postpone the choices held out to us
On every turn of the path we were on already.
No way to be sure we'd behave like characters
We admired when they confronted a challenge
Similar to our own, though not identical.
Just raising the question, she said, would be of use,

Along with the question, how lenient a book
Were we acting in. For our sake she hoped
It had room for a second chance if we failed
The first time, that its door didn't open
Just once and then shut for good.

Help from an Old Critic

It's a lonely job, telling a writer like you
That I don't regard the poem you've sent me
As the big improvement you think it is
Over the poems of yesteryear.

Lonely, but I have to reject your comparing it
To a garment made of cloth woven this morning
As opposed to garments bleached by the sun
And faded from countless washings.
I'm obliged to say that the older poems still studied
Possess a brightness yours won't equal
Unless you succeed, when you revise it,
In solving the problems I've noted in the margins.

I'm obliged by my calling to tell you
You didn't compose your poem while standing
On the shoulders of older poets,
Glimpsing a promised land they couldn't see.
You stood on the ground in fog,
Holding a candle like the one they held
As they looked for a place to rest in the wilderness.

It's my job to tell you I don't believe your poem
Takes us to places we've never been to.
It takes us to a little field we know already,
Close to the edge of a creeping desert.
All your hoeing and weeding will go for nothing
Unless rain falls as it does in older poems.
And after the rain the chance of hearing
The familiar cheep of a robin or sparrow
And the chirr of a few crickets, a few cicadas.

At Emily Dickinson's House

What I remember now of the rooms
Where she spent more than half her life
In self-imposed seclusion
Is her writing table, just two feet square,
Which made my massive desk at home
An embarrassment, an oafish boast
That the work I did there was monumental.
Her table: easy to move to a bedroom window
When she needed more light or another glimpse
Of the garden she loved to work in
When the weather permitted.
What a pleasure it must have been
To plant and prune in the afternoon
After a long morning at the table
Ample enough to serve as the field
Where she stepped out early to welcome Eden
Or rode alone to meet the enemy: the dark
That snuffed out her bright dear ones.
How much comfort she took in the hope
That the poems she didn't try to publish
Would cast a light one day is uncertain,
How much faith in a word as remote
And bloodless as *posterity*. I'd like to tell her
I've climbed the stairs in my heavy boots
To the room with the little table where once
She sat in her slippers, summoning her reserves
To charge "the cavalry of woe."

Babel

One useful lesson of the tale of Babel
Is that no language spoken today can boast
Of being the language Adam employed in Eden
When naming the animals as they passed
In a peaceable line before him.
One less reason for any nation to claim
Priority over all the others.

Too bad the tale also suggests that the many
Languages now available weren't intended
To delight us with their variety, just to disrupt
Work on the tower that men were raising
Floor by floor to the gates of heaven.

No mention is made in the story
Of how the exhausted soil of a hard-used language
Can be fertilized by imports from overseas,
Borrowings we needn't return
Like *shampoo* and *yogurt*, *paradise* and *pajamas*.
No mention of how delighted we feel
When others borrow from us, without asking,
The likes of *rubbernecking*, *roustabout*, and *raccoon*.

The wish to learn how borrowed words are pronounced
By native speakers has prompted many
To learn a language, to savor the sound
Of *cumin*, *coriander*, and *cardamom*
As they might be chanted in a poem on local spices
Or cried in an open market in Isfahan.

If the truth has been broken up among many languages,
Each word may contribute its own rare gift:

The word for silence, for instance, on a South Sea archipelago
That denotes the quiet that allows you to hear
The waves lapping against a slip on a balmy evening.

And a word from a distant mainland for the silence
That falls in a garden when the leaves stop rustling
And the birds stop chirping, as if expecting
Something they haven't heard before.

On the Radio

Maybe the old painter was simply trying
To give an unpredictable answer
To the young interviewer's predictable question,
"Would you like to be young again?"
When he replied, "When I was young,
I was a pig." Or maybe he was serious.

Too bad the interviewer, thrown off balance,
Instead of asking for elaboration,
Changed the subject, leaving us in the radio audience
To fill in the blanks ourselves.

When I was young, I seldom wanted
To praise the work of my fellow students
Or to offer advice when asked,
So much did I think of success
As a matter of besting the competition.

When I was young, I forced my moods
On the defenseless landscape, too full of myself
To hear what the landscape might have to say.

And the portraits I painted back then
Often looked down, aloof, on their subjects.
What a boor I was to depict my father as someone
Who had tried to be like his son but had failed,
Lacking the requisite talent and ambition.

When I was young, I thought that old age
Troubled only the careless, along with the few
Denied the portion of luck they deserved,

Like my aunt Rebecca, who brought me by streetcar,
Each Sunday when I was little, to the museum.

If I made a sketch of her when I was a student,
I neglected to save it. Now I have only memory
To bring back her look of calm assurance,
When she first showed me her favorite paintings,
That one day soon I would show her mine.

Another Horatio

After fifty evenings of playing the part of Horatio
As Shakespeare wrote it, isn't it natural
For a thoughtful actor to wonder how the evening
Might end if he added a few more lines?
Why not a speech in which Horatio,
Setting aside his usual deference
To his royal friend, points out that the air
Of the palace, thick with intrigue and suspicion,
Isn't the only air, that elsewhere
Wind from the sea flutters the curtains?

No guarantee, of course, that the extra sentences,
If delivered convincingly, will convince the prince
To try something different, like urging his uncle
To say farewell to the court and queen
And cloister himself for a life of penance.
But doesn't the effort seem worth a try?

On the evenings the extra lines are withheld
The play will continue to be a tragedy.
But when the lines are added, the end
Isn't predictable. Sometimes a little push
May make a difference when all seems lost.
What if a puff of wind happens to blow
Enough dust from a scene to reveal
A fork in the road not noticed before?
We know where the right-hand path
Will take us, Horatio says to Hamlet,
So this evening let's try the left.

Old Composer

He still gives his mornings to writing music,
Only now, as he sits at his desk by the piano,
At work on a quintet for strings and oboe,
The musicians he'd choose to perform it
No longer dwell among the living.
Now he'll have to settle for five unknowns
Who, considering how seldom his pieces
Are being performed these days, may still be children,
Unaware of the years of practice ahead of them
Before they're ready to play his music,
Whether they play for many in concert
Or just for themselves. Of course, if he thought the piece
Would never rise from the page even once
To fill a room, he'd finish it for the satisfaction
Of giving form to feelings that otherwise would vanish.
But without the hope of an audience, the piece
Might acquire the overtones of an elegy,
Whereas he's doing his best to make it joyful,
To dwell not on the happenstance of obscurity
But on the gifts that have come his way unasked.
And now that he's written the measures he'd hoped
To write this morning, it's time for his usual walk
Through the park and his usual stop at the grocery.
Today the shoppers will seem less hurried to him
Than they seem on days when his morning work
Has been disappointing. They'll be taking their time
As they look for healthy items that might please their children,
Including the child who rises early to practice
The oboe on loan from her middle school.
What a pleasure it is for the old composer
To picture her in her room in the attic
Lost in the music while trying to play

More softly than she does in the evening
So the sleep of the family is not disturbed.

To Whitman

Given how often your poems address your readers,
It doesn't seem unmannerly to address you,
Though you're mainly concerned with encouragement
And I don't presume to encourage you.

In your prose, it's true, you wonder sometimes
If America will ever become the land
Of free-spirited, great-hearted individuals
You long to believe in. But in your poems
You seem to assume that the day long hoped for
Is here at last for those willing to take to the road
Open before them with an open mind.

In your prose you sometimes seem lonely. In your poems
You're certain a reader like me will join you
As soon as he lets his senses guide him,
As soon as he learns to treat his body
Not as a servant but as a companion.

I'm not sure how you manage to bring it off,
Your claim to know much about me
I'm not aware of: your assurance, for instance,
In your "Sundown Poem," that just as you feel
Crossing on the ferry to Brooklyn,
So I will feel, however distant I am.
Just as you take delight in the crowds on deck,
In slanting light on the water, and wheeling seagulls,
So I will take delight when I stand back
From my particular story and look about me.

And when you seem to be speaking to someone
More prone to expansive moments than I am,

83

You pause to tell me you've had your share
Of the smaller kind: "It is not upon you alone
The dark patches fall. . . . I too knitted the old knot of contrariety,
Blabb'd, blush'd, resented, lied, stole, grudg'd."

To respond to your confidence, the least I can do
To bring you closer is to try imagining you—
After the ferry has docked and the sun has set—
In the grip of a mood less certain
As you wander home alone under feeble streetlamps
To a ramshackle district where people like you,
Without steady work, find lodging.

Is that you up ahead, climbing the outside stairs
To your two small rooms? Is that you
Resting awhile on the cot by the stove
As the day grows quiet, wondering
If anyone anywhere in the world
Is thinking of you at that very moment?

Then it's time to get up and turn to work
On the poem that boldly addresses me
Across generations, that wants to convince me
You've managed to free yourself once again
From feeling estranged and dispensable.

I'm not sure what's implied near the end
When you turn from me to exhort the sun
To shine on, the water to glitter, the gulls
To wheel over the boats on the river.
Maybe you're simply thanking them for existing.
Or maybe your praise is meant to exhort them

Not to grow older by a minute. Let their power
Be undiminished when they offer others
All that they've offered you.

A Landscape

This painting of a barn and barnyard near sundown
May be enough to suggest we don't have to turn
From the visible world to the invisible
In order to grasp the truth of things.
We don't always have to distrust appearances.
Not if we're patient. Not if we're willing
To wait for the sun to reach the angle
When whatever it touches, however retiring,
Feels invited to step forward
Into a moment that might seem to us
Familiar if we gave ourselves more often
To the task of witnessing. Now to witness
A barn and barnyard on a day of rest
When the usual veil of dust and smoke
Is lifted a moment and things appear
To resemble closely what in fact they are.

Old Story

I like hearing the story my friend likes telling
Of how his father helped him one night,
When he was a boy, begin to edge past
His fear of the dark. A story he's chosen
To lift from the flow of incidents and endow,
After many retellings, with weight and purpose
Till it's one of the founding myths of his tribe.
At least once a year he revisits the man and boy
Alone in the big lot behind the house
Three miles from town. Dusk has moved into night.
And again the father, as he stands by the porch,
Tells his son to proceed alone down the path
Just to the spot where he starts to feel frightened
And then come back to the porch where he's certain
To find his father waiting. And again the boy,
On his first attempt, reaches the toolshed.
And again on the next, he extends his venturing
To the chicken house, and then to the pear tree.
Back to his father he goes, then out
To the stand of hemlocks, till finally
The dark of the boundary fence floats into view.
I can call the story a votive candle
The son lights to his father's memory.
And now that the son is some twenty years
Older than his father was when he died,
I can call it another rehearsal for the night
When his own soul is compelled to leave his body
Behind forever and wander alone on a road
He doesn't recognize. No house up ahead,
But off to the side, among the trees,
The light of a campfire where strangers
Sit in a circle, each one introducing himself

By telling a story. And here's the story he'll offer,
The one that may earn him an invitation
To stay by the fire as long as he wants,
Not to move on before he's ready to tell
His story to others who may be glad to hear it
By another fire that's burning who knows where.

CARL DENNIS is the author of twelve previous works of poetry, as well as a collection of essays, *Poetry as Persuasion*. In 2000 he received the Ruth Lilly Poetry Prize for his contribution to American poetry. His 2001 collection, *Practical Gods*, won the Pulitzer Prize. He lives in Buffalo, New York.

JOHN ASHBERY
Selected Poems
Self-Portrait in a Convex Mirror

PAUL BEATTY
Joker, Joker, Deuce

JOSHUA BENNETT
The Sobbing School

TED BERRIGAN
The Sonnets

LAUREN BERRY
The Lifting Dress

PHILIP BOOTH
Lifelines: Selected Poems 1950–1999

JULIANNE BUCHSBAUM
The Apothecary's Heir

JIM CARROLL
Fear of Dreaming: The Selected Poems
Living at the Movies
Void of Course

ALISON HAWTHORNE DEMING
Genius Loci
Rope
Stairway to Heaven

CARL DENNIS
Another Reason
Callings
New and Selected Poems 1974–2004
Night School
Practical Gods
Ranking the Wishes
Unknown Friends

DIANE DI PRIMA
Loba

STUART DISCHELL
Dig Safe

STEPHEN DOBYNS
Velocities: New and Selected Poems:
1966–1992

EDWARD DORN
Way More West

ROGER FANNING
The Middle Ages

ADAM FOULDS
The Broken Word

CARRIE FOUNTAIN
Burn Lake
Instant Winner

AMY GERSTLER
Crown of Weeds
Dearest Creature
Ghost Girl
Medicine
Nerve Storm
Scattered at Sea

EUGENE GLORIA
Drivers at the Short-Time Motel
Hoodlum Birds
My Favorite Warlord

DEBORA GREGER
By Herself
Desert Fathers, Uranium Daughters
God
In Darwin's Room

Men, Women, and Ghosts
Western Art

TERRANCE HAYES
Hip Logic
How to Be Drawn
Lighthead
Wind in a Box

NATHAN HOKS
The Narrow Circle

ROBERT HUNTER
Sentinel and Other Poems

MARY KARR
Viper Rum

JACK KEROUAC
Book of Blues
Book of Haikus
Book of Sketches

JOANNA KLINK
Circadian
Excerpts from a Secret Prophecy
Raptus

JOANNE KYGER
As Ever: Selected Poems

ANN LAUTERBACH
Hum
If in Time: Selected Poems,
1975–2000
On a Stair
Or to Begin Again
Under the Sign

CORINNE LEE
Plenty

PHILLIS LEVIN
May Day
Mercury
Mr. Memory & Other Poems

PATRICIA LOCKWOOD
Motherland Fatherland
Homelandsexuals

WILLIAM LOGAN
Macbeth in Venice
Madame X
Rift of Light
Strange Flesh
The Whispering Gallery

ADRIAN MATEJKA
The Big Smoke
Map to the Stars
Mixology

MICHAEL MCCLURE
Huge Dreams: San Francisco and
Beat Poems

ROSE MCLARNEY
Its Day Being Gone

DAVID MELTZER
David's Copy: The Selected Poems of
David Meltzer

ROBERT MORGAN
Dark Energy
Terroir

CAROL MUSKE-DUKES
Blue Rose
An Octave Above Thunder

Red Trousseau
Twin Cities

ALICE NOTLEY
Certain Magical Acts
Culture of One
The Descent of Alette
Disobedience
In the Pines
Mysteries of Small Houses

WILLIE PERDOMO
The Essential Hits of Shorty Bon Bon

LIA PURPURA
It Shouldn't Have Been Beautiful

LAWRENCE RAAB
The History of Forgetting
Visible Signs: New and Selected
Poems

BARBARA RAS
The Last Skin
One Hidden Stuff

MICHAEL ROBBINS
Alien vs. Predator
The Second Sex

PATTIANN ROGERS
Generations
Holy Heathen Rhapsody
Quickening Fields
Wayfare

SAM SAX
Madness

ROBYN SCHIFF
A Woman of Property

WILLIAM STOBB
Absentia
Nervous Systems

TRYFON TOLIDES
An Almost Pure Empty Walking

SARAH VAP
Viability

ANNE WALDMAN
Gossamurmur
Kill or Cure
Manatee/Humanity
Structure of the World Compared
to a Bubble

JAMES WELCH
Riding the Earthboy 40

PHILIP WHALEN
Overtime: Selected Poems

ROBERT WRIGLEY
Anatomy of Melancholy and Other
Poems
Beautiful Country
Box
Earthly Meditations: New and
Selected Poems
Lives of the Animals
Reign of Snakes

MARK YAKICH
The Importance of Peeling Potatoes
in Ukraine
Unrelated Individuals Forming a
Group Waiting to Cross